DISCARD

The Library of
Future Weather and Climate

Storms
of the Future

Paul Stein

The Rosen Publishing Group, Inc.
New York

Published in 2001 by The Rosen Publishing Group, Inc.
29 East 21st Street, New York, NY 10010

Copyright © 2001 by The Rosen Publishing Group, Inc.

First Edition 2001

Library of Congress Cataloging-in-Publication Data

Stein, Paul, 1968–
Storms of the future / Paul Stein.
p. cm. — (Library of future weather and climate)
Includes bibliographical references and index.
ISBN 0-8239-3417-9 (lib. bdg.)
1. Global warming—Environmental aspects—Juvenile literature.
2. Climatic changes—Environmental aspects—Juvenile literature.
3. Severe storms—Juvenile literature. [1. Global warming. 2. Storms.
3. Climatic changes. 4. Climatology.] I. Title.
QC981.8.G56 S75 2001
363.738'742—dc21

2001000005

All temperatures in this book are in degrees Fahrenheit, except where specifically noted. To convert to degrees Celsius, or centigrade, use the following formula:

Celsius temperature = (5 ÷ 9) x (the temperature in Fahrenheit - 32)

Manufactured in the United States of America

Contents

Introduction

Most of the time in any given location, the weather goes about its ordinary, everyday business. Sunny and mild one day, rainy and cool the next. The hot and humid "dog days" of summer are oppressive and tiring. A crisp winter day, with the sharp bite of cold air in the lungs, is bracing. The seasons pass. An infinite variety of clouds drift by overhead, thin and thick, sometimes wispy, sometimes like cotton balls. Most of the time we pay little attention.

The flash of lightning and the boom of thunder change all that in an instant. Weather bursts into our lives, often unannounced, sometimes violent. A thunderstorm randomly spits 50,000 degree Fahrenheit lightning bolts through the sky, over our heads, around our homes. A snowstorm locks us inside, leaving us to peer out through frosted windows as howling winds pile billions of icy flakes into huge white dunes. Worse yet, the unstoppable approach of a hurricane forces us to evacuate our homes, leaving behind everything we own, joining the traffic jam moving inland. Or a tornado warning flashes on the television screen at night. Outside in the darkness we hear only the growing sound of thunder and rising wind in the trees. We head for the basement.

If our own experiences with violent weather, rare though they may be, were not enough, television continually reminds us that right now, somewhere on Earth, fierce weather is battering someone. Television stations send their reporters out into the stormy elements to give eyewitness updates. Blown by hurricane winds, soaked to the skin, or shivering in a blizzard, they bring the wrath of the sky live into our living rooms.

A television news anchor speaks of "El Niño-spawned storms." After a big snowfall along the East Coast, a newspaper headline reads "Blame Global Warming for the Blizzard." Sometimes, with visions of high winds and flooding rains fresh in our minds from TV and newspapers, we wonder if the weather is getting more extreme. Are storms becoming more violent and more frequent? What will the future bring?

This book explores storms. From hurricanes to thunderstorms to extratropical cyclones, we examine how storms fit in with the ever-changing weather machine. What causes the atmosphere to spin into a fury, or explode with lightning and thunder? We look at trends, and see whether there's any evidence that storms have been on the increase in recent years. Looking ahead, we discuss global warming

This satellite view of Hurricane Carlotta on June 21, 2000, the day of its peak intensity, shows the hurricane as a giant spiral with a clearly visible eye.

and how it might change the earth's climate. What effect will this have on the various kinds of storms in the future?

We will take a closer look at hurricanes. Of all the different kinds of storms, hurricanes seem to be most directly linked with large-scale changes in the atmosphere around the earth. For example, the number and strength of hurricanes churning in the Atlantic in any given year is influenced by natural events all the way from the Pacific Ocean to Africa. Scientists tracking these events think there may be some changes in the years ahead.

Storms are a natural part of the atmosphere. Many people wonder whether storms of the future will be more frequent or more damaging than today. But storms of the present are destructive enough. We'll conclude this book with information on the various kinds of severe weather advisories issued by meteorologists. And we'll review what to do when severe weather threatens your home.

1 Atmospheric Eruptions

One of the best places to see storms is in outer space. Twenty-two thousand miles above the surface of the earth, weather satellites keep a nonstop watch on the atmosphere. Looking down from above, these instrument-laden spacecraft take snapshots of the cloud patterns below and beam the data back to receiving stations on the ground.

From a satellite's point of view, weather systems in Earth's atmosphere take on the appearance of giant spirals and comma-shaped patterns of clouds. Spinning eddies and great whorls of air silently bend and twist around the planet. Near the equator, a speckled belt of cloudiness circles the globe like an earthly Milky Way. Every once in a while, a bright pinwheel-like vortex

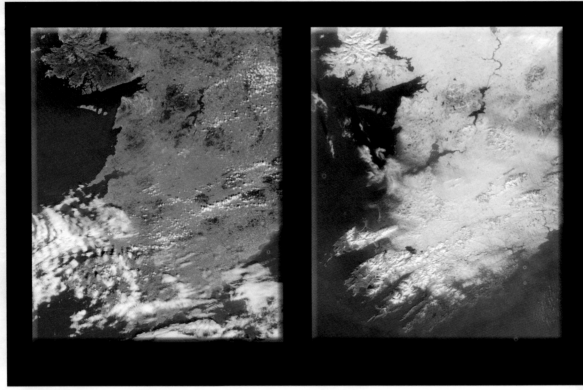

Ireland's climate is normally mild, but an uncommon cold snap between Christmas 1999 and New Year's Day 2000 dumped seven inches of snow on the Emerald Isle.

emerges from this splattering of clouds, seeming to take on a life of its own as it spins along.

The patterns of clouds seen by satellites show where the atmosphere is undergoing a rapid process of change. These are the storm systems, great whirlpools or eruptions of air that develop in regions where contrasting masses of air mix together. From the space-eye view far above Earth, we can distinguish three major types of storms.

The first are called extratropical cyclones, or extratropical storms, by meteorologists. These are the large, comma-shaped swirls of clouds that form and decay over a period of days. Extratropical storms are so-named because they occur outside of tropical regions, in areas where warm air from the Tropics mixes with cold air from the poles. Extratropical storms can cover hundreds of thousands of square miles and produce a wide variety of weather, including rain, snow, freezing rain, sleet, thunderstorms, and high winds.

An extratropical storm develops where large masses of air with contrasting temperatures, pressures, and densities meet. In between these contrasting air masses, winds accelerate at high altitudes in the atmosphere. These high-level "jet stream" winds help to trigger the formation of extratropical cyclones by removing air from over a region. With less air weighing down on the earth from above, surface air pressure falls.

Falling air pressure signals the formation of an extratropical cyclone. At ground level, winds blow in toward the center of low pressure and rise into the sky to replace the air that's removed by the jet stream. The rising air currents carry moisture high into the atmosphere where it forms clouds and precipitation, such as rain or snow. The rotation of Earth adds a spinning motion to the air, so that in the Northern Hemisphere, winds circulate in a counterclockwise direction as they spiral in toward the center of an extratropical cyclone.

This circulation draws warm, moist air into the storm on its east side, and cold, drier air into the storm on its west side. The leading edges of these warm and cold surges of air are marked by fronts, which serve as another focus for the formation of clouds and precipitation. The warm front usually extends to the east of the cyclone center, and is often accompanied by a broad area of steady precipitation. The cold front typically curves southward, and is often marked by a line of showery, sometimes heavy precipitation.

The strength of extratropical storms depends on the season. In the winter, the contrast increases between cold air moving toward the Tropics, and warm air moving toward the poles. This causes the jet stream to intensify and contributes to the formation of stronger storms. Powerful wintertime Pacific storms pound the West Coast of the United States. Blizzards bury the Plains states. Nor'easters lash the East Coast with rain, snow, and wind. In summer, on the other hand, the temperature contrast between the poles and the Tropics decreases. Extratropical storm systems become weaker.

As the weather grows warmer, however, conditions become more favorable for another, smaller kind of storm: the thunderstorm. From a satellite's perspective, thunderstorms appear as small, bright splotches of clouds scattered in clusters and lines across Earth. They can occur during any season, given the right conditions. But the warm, humid air of summer is the perfect environment for the formation of the towering thundercloud.

Thunderstorms and extratropical cyclones are often both referred to as "storms" by meteorologists, but they are two very different phenomena. Unlike extratropical cyclones, which can be hundreds of miles wide and cover a large portion of a country, a typical thunderstorm cloud is perhaps five miles in diameter and covers an area the size of a city. An extratropical cyclone lasts for days at a time, while an average thunderstorm may last for only a few hours.

Thunderstorms are basically an upheaval of the atmosphere, much like the boiling over of a pot of water on the stove. They form in relatively warm, humid weather when the difference in air temperature between ground level and high altitudes is considerable. If conditions are right, warmer air near the ground quickly rises tens of thousands of feet into

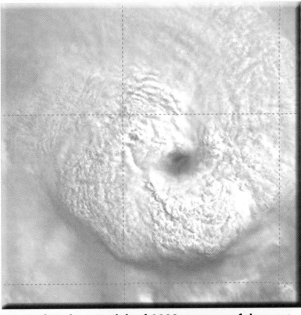

Tropical Cyclone Hudah of 2000 was one of the most powerful storms ever seen in the Indian Ocean.

the colder atmosphere, carrying abundant water vapor with it. Water vapor is just the invisible, gaseous form of water. As air rises, it cools, causing the water vapor to condense into billions of tiny cloud droplets that form the thunderstorm cloud. When water vapor condenses it adds energy to the air, fueling the storm and causing it to grow even bigger. The greater the temperature difference between low levels and high levels in the atmosphere, and the more water vapor available in the air, the larger the thunderstorm cloud can grow.

Thunderstorms often form in the heat of a summertime afternoon, as air warmed by the ground rises into the sky. Thunderstorms can also form along or ahead of the cold front that sweeps eastward around the south side of an extratropical cyclone. And in tropical

13

A driver caught in a storm is faced with low visibility because of the drenching rain and high winds.

regions, over the warm ocean water, thunderstorms can sometimes act as the seeds for a much larger, potentially very destructive kind of storm.

This third kind of storm is the tropical cyclone, which is just the meteorological name for a hurricane. In other parts of the world, tropical cyclones are called typhoons, or just cyclones. But they're all just different terms for the same kind of storm. From a weather satellite orbiting Earth, a well-developed tropical cyclone looks like a pinwheel of clouds surrounding a clear center, or "eye." It can be hundreds of miles wide and last for days or even weeks as it drifts along with the global flow of air, like a leaf in a river.

Tropical cyclones typically develop from clusters of thunderstorms over warm tropical ocean water. These thunderstorms are part of a zone of permanently unsettled weather that circles the globe near the equator. Meteorologists call this belt of clouds, showers, and thunderstorms the intertropical convergence zone, or ITCZ for short. It marks the region where tropical air flowing from the northeast clashes with tropical air flowing from the southeast.

Clusters of thunderstorms in the ITCZ march westward with the prevailing flow of air in the Tropics. As these atmospheric disturbances drift over the warm ocean water, some of them intensify. Air pressure at the surface of the ocean falls, and winds begin to spiral in toward the center of low pressure. The thunderstorm activity increases and becomes organized around the center of the cyclone. The lower the pressure falls in a tropical

This satellite photo shows the telltale spiral associated with a large extratropical cyclone, the so-called perfect storm, off the eastern seabord on October 30, 1991.

cyclone, the stronger it becomes and the faster the air spirals in toward the center of the storm. Winds in the strongest tropical cyclones can blow at 150 mph or more.

The warm, humid air of summer is the perfect environment for the formation of the towering, ominous-looking clouds of the thunderstorm.

For a tropical cyclone to develop, several conditions must exist. Tropical cyclones gain their energy from the warm waters of the tropical oceans. Ocean water temperatures must be 80 degrees Fahrenheit or higher for a tropical cyclone to develop. Also, large amounts of moisture must exist in the atmosphere to contribute to cloud formation. Unlike extratropical cyclones, winds in the upper levels of the atmosphere must be light over a developing tropical cyclone. This is because strong upper-level winds can shear the developing thunderstorms apart. However, like extratropical cyclones, upper-level winds must ventilate a developing tropical cyclone by removing air at high altitudes over the storm.

There are many other complex processes involved in the formation of storms. But essentially, storms can be thought of as the atmosphere's attempt to return to a state of order from a state of disorder. Since it's "normal" for the atmosphere to be disorderly, storms occur constantly around the earth in different locations. Sometimes these storms grab our attention, either by inflicting extraordinary damage in some other part of the world, or by passing right over our homes. Based on some extraordinary storms of recent years, many people are asking whether the atmosphere is getting more violent. It's a difficult question to answer.

2 Recording the Weather

The National Climatic Data Center (NCDC) in Asheville, North Carolina, is a national warehouse of historical climate data. Acting as the self-described "scorekeeper" of severe weather events across the United States, NCDC maintains a list of billion-dollar weather disasters. From droughts to tornadoes to hurricanes and winter storms, these are the extreme weather events that have struck the United States and caused $1 billion in damage or more.

Record drought withered the central United States in 1980. It happened again in 1988. Hurricane Andrew raked southern Florida in 1992. The Mississippi River burst its banks in 1993. Torrential rains flooded parts of the West Coast in the winter of 1996–1997. An ice storm paralyzed parts of the Northeast in 1998. These are

Hurricane Andrew's brutal winds reduced much of Homestead, Florida, to rubble in 1992 and caused billions of dollars worth of damage throughout southern Florida.

just some of the forty-eight extreme weather events since 1980 that, according to NCDC, have each inflicted over $1 billion in damages. Storms, in one form or another, account for around 75 percent of these extreme weather events.

"The list appears to show an ominous trend. Forty-one of the forty-eight disasters have occurred since 1988. While no year in the 1980s had more than three distinct billion-dollar weather disasters, all but two years in the 1990s had three or more. The peak year for weather disasters, at least through the year 2000, was 1998, when seven such events occurred."

There are, however, some reasons for the rise in costly disasters, other than stronger or more frequent storms. Increasing population, and the expansion of cities and suburbs, has put more people and property at risk for severe weather. In particular, development has sky-rocketed along hurricane-prone coastal regions. And the dollar value of these properties has risen by 150 to 250 percent in most states since 1980. Development in river flood plains has also increased dramatically. The population and its wealth are growing. A storm that caused half a billion dollars in damage thirty years ago might cause a billion-and-a-half today.

Looking for trends in the frequency and intensity of storms is not a straightforward business. Meteorologists examine years of weather records looking for patterns in the changing weather. Weather records are the data that scientists use to make judgments about what's currently taking place in the atmosphere. The data comes from the

A meteorologist examines equipment at the meteorological station in São Miguel, Azores.

observations taken at thousands of weather stations worldwide. People measure temperature, humidity, pressure, rainfall, snowfall, and wind on an hourly basis, twenty-four hours per day, all year long, all around the world.

Examining these kinds of weather records over a period of years, scientists try to assess which way the weather is headed. In the case of temperatures across the world, it's been a relatively easy task. Data from weather observations show that the average temperature of the earth has risen at least one degree Fahrenheit over the course of the twentieth century. And scientists have been able to refine this observation. The data show that nighttime temperatures have warmed faster than daytime temperatures. And high-latitude weather stations—in

Canada and Russia, for example—have warmed more than weather stations in the Tropics.

But looking for trends in the frequency and intensity of storms is a more complicated matter. For one thing, a storm's strength can be measured in different and contradictory ways. For example, the amount of rain or snow that a weather observer records during a storm may depend on the storm's overall intensity. But it also depends on the speed at which the storm is moving. A slow-moving, weaker storm may drop more rain or snow at a given location than a much stronger, faster-moving storm. It's also not the case that the bigger the storm, the more powerful it is. In fact, some of the more intense hurricanes are also relatively small.

Another problem is that scientists need as complete a set of data as possible to make accurate observations. The greater the number of weather stations the better. The farther back in time those stations have been observing weather the better. A weather station that's been faithfully recording data for 100 years is better than one that's only been around for 10 years, assuming that the people recording the data have been doing so reliably and with accurate instruments. Across the earth, relatively few countries have been recording weather for more than a century. And large parts of the world lack weather observations altogether. Trying to establish global trends for storms is like trying to visualize the picture on a jigsaw puzzle when only a few pieces are in place.

Another factor concerns the interpretation of the data. If data show that storms appear to be getting stronger or more frequent, scientists

Meteorologists use supercomputers like this Cray model to crunch weather data and make forecasts.

must ask why. They must look behind the numbers. A good example of this is the trend in the increasing frequency of billion-dollar weather disasters in the United States. Another reminder of the importance in interpreting the data comes when we look at the number of tornadoes recorded in the United States during the twentieth century.

In the early 1950s, when meteorologists first began recording the annual tornado frequency, they tallied 200 to 300 tornadoes per year. By the 1990s, the annual number of tornadoes in the United States had risen to over 1,000! It appears as though there is a significant upward trend in the number of tornadoes striking the United States.

However, let's dig deeper. One of the reasons for the upward trend has to do with how tornadoes are being observed and recorded. In the 1950s, there was no reliable system people could use to document whether a tornado had touched down. Across the wide-open Plains of the central United States, where most of these storms occur, there are no humans around for miles. Many tornadoes went unrecorded. And if someone did observe a tornado but did not communicate that observation to the authorities, the tornado touchdown would never be tallied.

The National Weather Service uses Doppler radar stations to measure the speed and intensity of storms.

Gradually, through the decades, this has all changed. Today, organized groups of weather watchers called "storm spotters" closely monitor thunderstorms for tornado activity. They often drive to the location of the storm, even if it's far out in a rural area, miles from any town. Meteorologists make detailed surveys of storms after the fact, to find out if indeed a tornado has touched down. And Doppler radar, a weather-sensing instrument not yet developed back in the 1950s, is now able to pinpoint the swirling winds inside a thunderstorm that may lead to a tornado. Meteorologists can see where Doppler radar indicates a possible tornado, then follow up with a storm survey the next day. Mostly because of these factors, along with an increasing

This is a satellite image of a typhoon in Australia.

public awareness of tornadoes, the number of reported tornadoes in the United States has risen by well over 300 percent since the 1950s.

Turning to tropical cyclones, scientists find a relatively complete and reliable data set for examination. Meteorologists have kept records on the number and intensity of Atlantic hurricanes all the way back to the start of the twentieth century. Over the last thirty years or so, an average of around nine tropical cyclones have formed in the Atlantic each year. Typically, between five and six of these tropical cyclones go on to become full-blown hurricanes. In the mid- and late-1990s, above-average tropical cyclone activity raised questions. Are tropical cyclones becoming more frequent or more intense?

Looking at hurricane trends across the entire Atlantic, many meteorologists think there have been some changes. One 1999 study tracked Atlantic and East Coast hurricanes during the twentieth century and found that the frequency of hurricanes had increased since the 1970s. The years from 1995 through 1998 saw thirty-three hurricanes, a record for any four-year period dating back to the 1940s. The scientific consensus is that the number of intense hurricanes in the Atlantic has increased in recent years.

However, a 1998 study by researchers at Florida State University looked at the number of hurricanes crossing the Gulf Coast, from Texas to Florida, from 1896 to 1995. They found that there was no overall increase in the frequency of these "landfalling" tropical cyclones during this period. And the decade from 1986 to 1996 actually saw the fewest number of intense hurricanes (with winds of 110 mph or more) in a century.

Elsewhere, trends are mixed. Around Australia, for example, research has shown an overall decrease in the annual number of moderate and strong tropical cyclones since 1970. In the northwest Pacific Ocean, on the other hand, tropical cyclones (called typhoons in that part of the world) have been on the increase since 1980.

Trends are a tricky business. While some devastating storms have struck various parts of the world recently, stormy weather is a normal part of the ever-changing atmosphere. Bearing in mind the problems that meteorologists face when searching for a pattern in the number and strength of storms, we next look to what the future might bring.

3 Winds of Change

In late December 1999, residents and tourists in Paris, France, were enjoying the festive holiday season. Like people all around the world, Parisians were making the final preparations for the millennium celebration, the long-awaited, once-in-a-thousand-years party. The city was expecting tens of thousands of visitors to fill its famous boulevards on New Year's Eve, and to gather around the famous Eiffel Tower for a grand fireworks display at midnight.

Christmas Day dawned peacefully across France, as most people stayed at home with family and friends. Few people were aware of events taking place high in the cold, thin air over the North Atlantic, a thousand miles away. Meteorologists, however, were becoming concerned about a powerful extratropical cyclone predicted by computer

Days before the millennium celebration in Paris in December 1999, the most powerful storm in France's recorded history ripped thousands of trees up by the roots with winds of over 100 mph.

models to sweep southeastward from the open ocean waters. As the computer predictions began to come true, winds started to accelerate over the ocean west of France on Christmas night. The storm intensified, taking aim at western Europe. Clouds thickened over the quiet, tree-lined streets and empty cafés of Paris.

Thousands of people all across France woke early on Sunday the 26th to the sound of shattering glass and splintering trees. The most powerful storm in France's recorded history had crashed onshore and was sweeping across the country. Winds blasted the French coastline at over 120 mph. In Paris, torrential rain sent flood waters surging from the Seine River into city streets. Gusts over 100 mph whipped around city buildings and through parks, ripping hundreds of trees up by the roots. Another 60,000 trees were blown flat in forests just outside Paris. Ten miles away, the gardens around the great Palace of Versailles were devastated, with the carnage of 10,000 trunks littering the grounds. Some of the fallen trees had withstood storms since the time of Napoleon. Millions of homes across the country lost power. Over forty people died in France. And just two days later, another violent storm battered many of the same areas with gales and heavy rain. Across Europe, the storms of December 1999 killed over 120 people.

The storms that battered Europe just before the turn of the century were not the only extraordinary weather events of 1999. In mid-December, flash floods and mudslides devastated coastal regions of Venezuela in South America. Tens of thousands died as whole towns were engulfed in rocks, water, and debris. The worst flooding in a

The aftermath of flash floods and mudslides in the state of Vargas, Venezuela.

century struck Vietnam in November and December, driving a million people from their homes and drowning 700. In October, thousands perished in India when two tropical cyclones, one of which was the strongest ever recorded in that part of the world, struck the eastern coast of the country. In the United States, Hurricane Floyd caused billions of dollars in damage in mid-September as it unleashed catastrophic river flooding from North Carolina to New Jersey. In Oklahoma in early May, the largest tornado outbreak of that state's history killed dozens of people and leveled whole neighborhoods in Oklahoma City.

The stormy weather of 1999 was an ominous way to end the century at a time when worldwide climate was changing at a pace not seen in centuries. Year after year in the 1990s, scientists tracking the changing climate tallied warmer and warmer weather across the planet. The year 1999 was the twenty-first consecutive year that the global mean temperature was higher than the long-term average. The ten warmest years in recorded history, dating back nearly a century and a half, all occurred since the early 1980s. And scientists think that the 1990s were most likely the warmest decade in the last 1,000 years.

Blame for the global temperature rise is usually assigned to the increasing levels of greenhouse gases in the atmosphere. Greenhouse gases, such as carbon dioxide, are particularly efficient absorbers of radiation released by the earth. Radiation is just a form of energy, consisting of invisible electromagnetic waves. The more of this energy the atmosphere absorbs, the more it emits back down to the earth. This natural back-and-forth exchange of energy between the atmosphere and the earth is known as the greenhouse effect, and it acts as a kind of global thermostat, maintaining the earth's life-sustaining climate. But when greenhouse gas levels increase, as they do through the burning of coal, natural gas, and oil, so too does this natural thermostat setting. The result is a warmer planet.

Global warming poses major threats, including sea level rise, drought, and climate-related effects on plant and animal life. Scientists now estimate that the earth's average temperature may rise anywhere from three to nearly eleven degrees Fahrenheit by the end of the twenty-first century. That's a magnitude of warming greater than the world has seen in the last 10,000 years. Many people wonder what effect this drastic change in climate will have on storms.

When it comes to global warming and hurricanes, the link seems clear. Tropical cyclones feed on warm ocean water. The warmer the world becomes in the future, the higher the temperature of the oceans. This appears to indicate that hurricanes will become stronger, possibly more frequent, and more widespread as the area of ocean water warm enough for tropical cyclone formation expands in size.

But scientists aren't so sure. Recall from chapter 2 that it takes more than just warm water to form a tropical cyclone. The global circulation of air sets up a stormy zone in the Tropics, known as the ITCZ, which serves as a breeding ground for tropical cyclones. However, the same circulation of air creates a zone of calm weather in the subtropics, around thirty degrees north and south latitude, which is unfavorable for tropical cyclones. Air tends to sink and spread apart in this area, a process that prevents tropical cyclones from forming.

Therefore, the relatively stable pattern of global air circulation sets natural limits to the formation of tropical cyclones. Even if ocean water warms considerably in subtropical regions, sinking and spreading air-flow in the atmosphere over these parts of the world would still prevent tropical cyclone formation. And there's no evidence that global warming would shift or alter the global flow of air that creates these favorable and unfavorable zones.

Scientists are similarly skeptical about the frequency of tropical cyclones, commonly known as hurricanes, in a warmer world. Some

Because tropical cyclones feed on warm ocean water, some scientists predict stronger storms in the future as a result of global warming.

have speculated that rising temperatures in the upper levels of the atmosphere may even act to reduce the numbers of hurricanes. Warmer upper-level air would decrease the temperature contrast between the surface of the earth and high altitudes. As we saw in chapter 2, thunderstorms form in areas where this vertical temperature difference is relatively strong. With a weaker temperature contrast from high levels to low levels in the atmosphere, thunderstorms become less frequent and so do the hurricanes that sometimes come from them.

However, there is a possibility that warmer ocean water may contribute to an overall increase in the intensity of hurricanes, though not by much. Meteorologists run computer simulations of the atmosphere to predict how tropical cyclones will behave if global warming proceeds as predicted. Computers predict that air pressure at the centers of tropical cyclones may fall by 10 to 20 percent in a world where carbon dioxide levels are doubled from present values. In general, the lower the central pressure of a tropical cyclone, the stronger it is. A 10 to 20 percent reduction in air pressure translates into a 5 to 10 percent increase in hurricane wind speed. In other words, a hurricane that blows at 100 mph today might blow at 110 mph fifty or a hundred years from now.

Tropical cyclones depend on ocean water for their strength. Extratropical cyclone intensity, by contrast, is less easy to pin down. It relates to the difference in temperature between colliding masses of warm and cold air. The sharper the temperature contrast, the faster jet stream winds blow and the stronger the extratropical storm may become. In other words, cold air plays just as important a role in determining the strength of an extratropical cyclone as warm air.

A warmer world, therefore, will not necessarily contribute to stronger extratropical storms. In fact, scientists can argue that a warmer planet may reduce average extratropical cyclone intensity. Just look at what happens each summer as the temperature difference decreases between the warm Tropics and the cold poles. The jet stream weakens and extratropical cyclones become less severe. Global warming may well work in the same way. Climatologists who look far back in time note that cold periods, not warm periods, seem to have been the stormiest times on our planet. Evidence suggests that ice ages sharpened temperature contrasts and generated high winds that lofted large amounts of dust into the air. Warmer periods in between ice ages have had their share of storms, but may be less stormy on average.

One thing does seem clear as global warming proceeds through the twenty-first century: Storms will likely get wetter. The reason has to do with evaporation rates. Evaporation occurs as liquid water is transformed into gaseous water vapor. In general, the higher the temperature, the higher the rate of evaporation and the more water vapor gathers in the atmosphere. With more atmospheric moisture to tap, storms of the future may very well produce heavier rain and snow. As a result, flooding may be on the increase in the decades to come. One study published by a meteorologist at the National Climatic Data Center in 1998 showed that the number of days with especially heavy rainfall has been increasing in the United States through the twentieth century. Little research has been conducted in other countries.

So while the evidence is rapidly mounting that global warming may contribute to a change in climate unlike any seen in thousands of years, the link between global warming and storms remains unclear. However, we need to take another look at hurricanes. Some researchers think we may be entering a new era of increased hurricane activity in the Atlantic Ocean, completely unrelated to global warming. In the next chapter, we examine this threat.

4 Return of the Hurricanes

Late in September 1995, meteorologists were closely tracking a cluster of thunder-storms moving westward over the Yucatán Peninsula of Mexico. In fact, these thunderstorms were part of a weather system spawned some three weeks earlier by the ITCZ over western Africa. Day after day, thunderstorms formed, dissipated, and re-formed within the weak weather system as it drifted steadily from east to west across the Atlantic Ocean.

It wasn't until the tropical weather system had reached Mexico, some 4,500 miles from its starting point, that the thunderstorms finally began to organize around an area of low air pressure at the surface of

From June to November, residents along the Gulf Coast are constantly on the lookout for hurricanes.

the earth. Around dawn on September 30, as the winds circulating in toward the low-pressure area reached a speed of around forty mph, the system became a tropical storm and was given a name: Opal. Tropical Storm Opal drifted into the southern Gulf of Mexico and continued to strengthen.

On October 2, hurricane-hunter aircraft flying through the storm verified that winds in Opal had increased to 74 mph, classifying it as a hurricane. Opal began to turn toward the north and head in the direction of the U.S. Gulf Coast. On the morning of October 3, forecasters at the National Hurricane Center in Florida issued a hurricane watch for parts of the Gulf Coast, including the Florida Panhandle. Residents began boarding up homes and readying emergency supplies. On the evening of October 3, people watching the evening news in the Florida Panhandle were informed that Opal was continuing to strengthen gradually, with winds reaching over 100 mph. It looked as though Opal would cross the coastline sometime late the next day.

Most residents were concerned, though some took the news in stride. While a 100-mph hurricane is life-threatening and capable of doing significant damage, it ranks only a two on the five-point Saffir-Simpson Hurricane Scale for hurricane strength. Floridians had ridden out similar storms in the past. And many folks could remember hurricanes that threatened the coast, only to turn away. Most people along the coast from Mobile, Alabama, to Apalachicola, Florida, went to bed that night planning to drive inland the next day, allowing plenty of time before the category-two storm crossed the coast.

Then, in the darkness of night out over the warm water of the Gulf of Mexico, while people slept, Opal became a monster. Panhandle residents were horrified when they woke the morning of the 4th. Overnight, in only a few hours, Opal's winds had strengthened to 150 mph. It was a shade away from reaching category-five strength, the most powerful type of hurricane known. It was more powerful than Hurricane Andrew was when it smashed into south Florida in 1992, causing $20 billion in damage. And it was accelerating toward the coast.

In a panic, people across the Florida Panhandle jumped into their cars and headed inland. Roads quickly became clogged. Cars inched along in a traffic jam that moved in agonizing starts and stops. Frightened motorists packed gas stations trying to fill up before the storm hit. Rain squalls along the outer edges of the 300-mile wide hurricane moved onshore during the late morning and overspread the crawling traffic.

As the first rain-soaked gusts of wind drenched the crush of vehicles heading inland, it became clear that the approaching hurricane was overtaking the evacuation. Emergency officials had seen enough. They ordered all cars off the roads and highways, forcing people to take shelter where they could. Just after authorities cleared cars from Interstate 10, a tornado spun out of one of the rain squalls and skipped across the highway. One person was killed by the twister as it smashed a mobile home nearby.

Luckily, Hurricane Opal weakened just as fast as it intensified. It crossed the Florida Panhandle late in the afternoon of October 4, with sustained winds of 110 mph—much reduced from its peak strength just hours earlier. But that was bad enough. Oceanside homes were smashed to bits by pounding waves. Roofs were peeled from buildings. Trees and power lines snapped. Rivers overflowed. Fortunately, there were relatively few deaths from the hurricane. But total damage from Opal across the southeastern United States was in the billions of dollars.

Opal serves as a lesson in the unpredictability of hurricanes. It also gives warning that next time people might not be so lucky. After flexing its muscles out in the Gulf of Mexico, Opal crossed the

Floridians, following orders to evacuate coastal areas, head inland to avoid the predicted fury of Hurricane Opal.

coast as a weakening hurricane. Had it maintained strength, or even continued to intensify, the cost would have been much greater. Had Opal smashed into the Florida Panhandle as the category-five storm it threatened to be, hundreds might have died.

Some of the best hurricane researchers in the United States worry that such a scenario will one day happen. They worry that in the future another hurricane will once again rapidly (and perhaps unexpectedly) intensify, and accelerate toward the coast. People will be caught off guard, just as they were with Opal. The evacuation will be rushed and panicky. And, unlike Opal, the nightmare hurricane of the future will blast onshore at full strength.

Adding to the potential hurricane disaster of the future is beach-front development. For years, hurricane experts have warned that coastal regions are being overbuilt. What once were miles of sparsely populated beaches and islands are now areas crowded with roads, hotels, condominiums, houses, and businesses. People love the ocean and love to live and vacation near it. But building along the ocean involves risk and increases the potential for catastrophe.

Part of the problem is that a scarcity of intense hurricanes (with winds of 110 mph or more) in recent decades may have lulled people into a false sense of security. Researchers think that hurricane activity in the Atlantic rises and falls over a period of twenty to thirty years. Since around 1970, Atlantic hurricane activity has been on the low side. Before that however, from the mid-1940s to the late 1960s, intense hurricanes were much more common in the Atlantic.

This rising and falling hurricane cycle is caused by the global circulation of ocean water. Large ocean currents, sometimes thousands of miles long and hundreds of miles wide, drift along at a few miles per hour both on the surface of the world's oceans and deep underwater. These ocean currents help distribute warm and cold water toward the poles and the equator. The Gulf Stream is one example of an ocean current. It carries warm, tropical water northeastward from near Florida all the way to northern Europe.

Ocean currents have a major impact on weather patterns. Warm ocean currents heat the air above them, while cold ocean currents absorb heat from the air. Large masses of air can warm or cool as a result of changing ocean temperatures underneath them. Recall that changes in temperature lead to changes in air pressure and wind speed. And oceans also affect the moisture content of the air: warmer ocean water evaporates faster, leading to higher humidity. More humidity means more clouds and rainfall.

Scientists have been able to link the speed of the Atlantic Ocean circulation to changes in weather patterns that affect hurricane development. In a complex chain of cause and effect, weak ocean circulation leads to stronger winds and higher air pressure off the west coast of Africa. This tends to prevent the formation of hurricanes, since strong winds shear developing thunderstorms apart. Strong winds also contribute to a cooling of ocean water in the tropical Atlantic by pushing water much faster toward the west on the surface of the ocean. As the water is pushed away, cold water rises from beneath to take its place. Cold water is unfavorable for hurricane development.

This weak circulation scenario dominated the Atlantic from 1970 to the mid-1990s, thereby contributing to the relative lack of tropical cyclones during that time. However, scientists now see a change. They think the Atlantic Ocean circulation is accelerating once again, and that this will lead to weather pattern changes that will favor the development of more and stronger hurricanes. Recent increased hurricane activity in the mid- and late 1990s seem to be pointing in this direction.

Dr. William M. Gray, a professor at Colorado State University, is one of the leading tropical weather experts in the United States. He has

Hurricane forecaster William Gray addresses the general session at the fourteenth Annual Governor's Hurricane Conference in Tampa, Florida, on May 26, 2000.

spent considerable effort studying the kinds of weather patterns that influence hurricane development. Gray and his team of researchers look at Atlantic Ocean water circulation, wind patterns over the Atlantic, rainfall amounts in western Africa, ocean water temperatures, and many other factors. Dr. Gray has become famous for issuing a yearly prediction of Atlantic tropical-cyclone activity based on these factors.

Looking farther into the future, Dr. Gray appears deeply concerned about the potential for an increase in hurricane activity and intensity over the Atlantic Ocean. In a paper submitted to the 10th Symposium on Global Change Studies, held by the American Meteorological Society in Dallas, Texas, in 1999, Gray was blunt. "I view this growing hurricane threat to be our country's greatest natural hazard," he wrote, "more than earthquakes; more than floods, tornadoes, extreme temperatures, global warming, etc." Gray warned of a "new era" of intense hurricane activity in the Atlantic Ocean. "If our interpretation of climate trends which are indicating increased intense hurricane activity bear out," Gray warned, "then the cost of U. S. hurricane-spawned destruction will be of a magnitude as never before seen."

Conclusion

Storms are naturally occurring events in the earth's atmosphere. It's normal for the weather to be stormy, at least some of the time. Recent destructive storms around the world have caused people to wonder whether the atmosphere is getting more violent. Global warming, caused by increasing levels of greenhouse gases in the atmosphere, adds to the controversy.

Extratropical cyclones and thunderstorms may be getting wetter as the warming atmosphere gains humidity. However, there's no evidence yet that winter storms, tornadoes, or extratropical cyclones have been growing more powerful over time. Despite the lack of evidence, however, the future remains uncertain. Global warming seems likely to change the earth's climate in ways never before experienced by human beings. Weather patterns may shift in unexpected ways, and storms will likely change along with the weather. It's possible that global warming could bring a stormier future, but it also may lead to weaker storms. The evidence from history points towards the second possibility as the more likely scenario. Storms may drop more rain and snow on average, but may be weaker overall. There's no way to be sure just yet.

Hurricanes, however, may have an agenda of their own that has little or nothing to do with global warming. Changes in the Atlantic Ocean circulation occurring every few decades or so result in weather conditions that can either spawn or suppress hurricanes. Some of the leading hurricane researchers in the United States think that we may be entering a new phase of increased hurricane severity. With the recent coastal development over the last few decades, the potential for catastrophe is growing.

No matter what the future brings, and no matter where in the world people live, storms will remain a threat to life and property. The best way to prepare for the unpredictable nature of storms is to know what to do when severe weather strikes. Learning about storms can make them less frightening and can inspire respect. Storms can be exciting, but knowing their dangers may one day save your life, or the lives of others.

Storm Safety

What follows is a list of basic storm-safety rules, along with an explanation of various severe weather advisories issued by the National Weather Service.

Hurricanes

A hurricane watch means that hurricane conditions are possible in the watch area, typically within thirty-six hours. Hurricane conditions include winds of 74 mph or higher, flooding rains, and a potentially deadly flood of ocean water along the coast known as storm surge.

A hurricane warning means that hurricane conditions are expected in the warning area, typically within twenty-four hours. Follow instructions from adults, and be prepared to evacuate if the hurricane threatens your area.

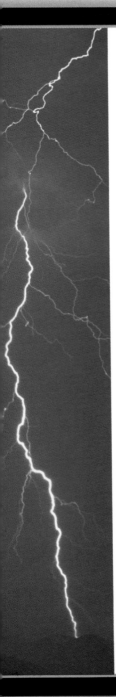

Tornadoes

A tornado watch means that conditions are favorable for the development of tornadoes in and close to the watch area. Remain calm, but be alert to rapidly changing weather conditions.

A tornado warning is much more serious. It means that a tornado has actually been spotted, or is being tracked by weather radar. Leave cars and mobile homes and get inside a sturdy building. Go to the basement. If a basement is not available, get inside a closet or bathroom in the middle of the building on the lowest floor. If in school, crouch down in an interior hallway. Get out of auditoriums, cafeterias, libraries, or any other extra-large rooms. The large ceilings in these rooms are especially prone to collapse in tornado winds.

Severe Thunderstorms

A severe thunderstorm watch means that severe thunderstorms are possible in and near the watch area. Severe thunderstorms produce any of the following: damaging winds, large hail, flooding rains, dangerous lightning, and tornadoes.

A severe thunderstorm warning means that severe thunderstorms are actually occurring in the warned area. Seek shelter inside a sturdy building, away from doors and windows. Stay off the telephone, and avoid using sinks or bathroom plumbing. If in school, get out of auditoriums, cafeterias, libraries, or any other extra-large rooms.

Lightning

When lightning threatens, get inside. Stay off the telephone and avoid using sinks or bathroom plumbing. If caught outside with no building available, seek shelter in a car. Do not seek shelter from the storm under a tree. Trees and other tall objects naturally attract lightning.

Winter Storms

A winter-storm watch means that a winter storm is possible in the watch area, usually within thirty-six hours. A winter storm can be accompanied by any of the following: heavy snow, sleet, or freezing rain; strong winds; and dangerously low temperatures.

A winter-storm warning means that a winter storm is likely in the warned area, usually within twenty-four hours. During a winter storm, it's best to stay inside. If trapped in a car, do not try to walk to safety. Run the motor and heat the car ten minutes in every hour, and keep a window cracked to prevent dangerous exhaust fumes from building up inside. If possible, tie a brightly colored cloth to the car's antenna or to a windshield wiper. Try to keep the car's exhaust pipe clear of snow. Keep moving to stay warm.

A blizzard warning is issued when strong winds of 35 mph or more combine with heavy falling snow or blowing snow to severely reduce visibility for three hours or more. Safety precautions are the same as those for a winter-storm warning. The combination of strong winds and low temperatures that occur in a blizzard are particularly dangerous and increase the risk of frostbite to any exposed skin.

Floods

A flood watch, or flash-flood watch, means that flooding or flash flooding is possible in the watch area. Flooding and flash flooding are both life-threatening. Flash flooding is particularly dangerous, because water levels can rise in a matter of seconds.

A flood warning or flash-flood warning means that flooding or flash flooding is occurring, or likely to occur very soon, in the warned area. Stay away from streams, creeks, and rivers. Seek higher ground. Never drive through a flooded road. The water may be much deeper than it appears. Many flash-flood deaths occur in automobiles swept away by surging water.

Glossary

air mass   A large area of air at a similar temperature and humidity. An air mass can cover hundreds of thousands of square miles and extend tens of thousands of feet upward into the atmosphere.

climate   The average weather conditions over a long period of time, generally decades or more.

computer model   Complex computer software that simulates the behavior of the atmosphere and oceans and how they change over time.

condensation The process whereby invisible, gaseous water vapor changes into liquid water.

evaporation The process whereby liquid water changes into invisible, gaseous water vapor.

extratropical cyclone An area of low pressure outside the Tropics, typically accompanied by widespread clouds and precipitation, including either rain, snow, sleet, freezing rain, or any combination of the four.

greenhouse effect The naturally occurring process whereby the earth is warmer than it otherwise would be because of the presence of the atmosphere. Without the greenhouse effect, the earth would be devoid of life. Certain gases, including carbon dioxide, contribute to the greenhouse effect.

greenhouse gases Any gases that efficiently absorb outgoing radiation from the earth, thereby contributing to the greenhouse effect. The main greenhouse gases are water vapor, carbon dioxide, methane, nitrous oxide, chlorofluorocarbons, and ozone.

global warming The warming of the planet due to increasing amounts of greenhouse gases in the atmosphere.

hurricane The name used to describe a tropical cyclone in the Atlantic or eastern Pacific with winds of 74 mph or more.

intertropical convergence zone (ITCZ) A zone of unsettled weather in the Tropics that extends around the earth near the equator.

jet stream A discontinuous, fast-moving current of air high in the atmosphere at altitudes of 25,000 feet or more.

meteorologist A scientist who studies the weather.

radiation Energy in the form of invisible electromagnetic waves that travel at the speed of light

tropical cyclone An area of low pressure over tropical ocean water, accompanied by organized bands of thunderstorms and a counterclockwise circulating air flow. Hurricane, typhoon, tropical storm, and tropical depression are various names given to tropical cyclones of different strengths in different parts of the world.

tropical depression   The name used to describe a tropical cyclone in the Atlantic or eastern Pacific with winds less than 39 mph.

tropical storm   The name used to describe a tropical cyclone in the Atlantic or eastern Pacific with winds from 39 to 73 mph.

typhoon   The name used to describe a tropical cyclone in the western Pacific with winds of 74 mph or more.

water vapor   The invisible, gaseous form of water.

For More Information

American Meteorological Society (AMS)
45 Beacon St.
Boston, MA 02108-3693
http://www.ametsoc.org/AMS/
The AMS is the premiere professional
meteorological organization in the
United States.

National Hurricane Center (NHC)
11691 SW 17th Street
Miami, FL 33165-2149
http://www.nhc.noaa.gov/
On the National Hurricane Center Web
site, you can find the latest information on
tropical cyclone activity in the Atlantic
and eastern Pacific Oceans, as well as historical hurricane information.

National Climatic Data Center (NCDC)
Federal Building
151 Patton Avenue
Asheville NC 28801-5001
http://www.ncdc.noaa.gov/
Check out the NCDC's list of billion-dollar weather disasters, and read about other historical storms.

Storm Prediction Center (SPC)
1313 Halley Avenue
Norman, Oklahoma 73069
http://www.nssl.noaa.gov/spc/
The Storm Prediction Center is tasked with forecasting for severe thunderstorms and tornadoes across the United States. They also issue bulletins on winter storms and other weather phenomena.

Weatherwise Magazine
Heldref Publications
1319 18th Street NW
Washington, DC 20036-1802
http://www.weatherwise.org/
A popular magazine about all things weather. Find it at your local library or newsstand.

For Further Reading

Allaby, Michael. *A Chronology of Weather.* New York: Facts on File, 1998.

Allaby, Michael. *Blizzards* (Facts on File Dangerous Weather Series). New York: Facts on File, 1997.

Allaby, Michael. *Droughts* (Facts on File Dangerous Weather Series). New York: Facts on File, 1997.

Allaby, Michael. *Floods* (Facts on File Dangerous Weather Series). New York: Facts on File, 1998.

Allaby, Michael. *Hurricanes* (Facts on File Dangerous Weather Series). New York: Facts on File, 1997.

Newson, Leslie. *Devastation! The World's Worst Natural Disasters.* New York: Dorling Kindersley, 1998.

Stevens, William K. *The Change in the Weather: People, Weather, and the Science of Climate.* New York: Delacorte Press, 1999.

Williams, Jack. *The Weather Book.* 2nd ed. New York: Vintage Books, 1997.

Index

About the Author

Paul Stein has a B.S. in meteorology from Pennsylvania State University. He has eight years experience as a weather forecaster, most recently as a senior meteorologist for The Weather Channel. Currently he develops computer systems and software that display and process weather-related data.

Photo Credits

Cover image © A.T. Willett/Image Bank: tornado on New Mexico high country.
Cover inset © SeaWIFS Project, NASA/GSFC and Orbimage: Typhoon Saomai.
Front matter and and back matter background © Weatherstock: storm clouds.
Introduction background © Weatherstock: lightning.
Chapter 1 background © FPG International: hurricane viewed from space.
Chapter 2 background © AP/Worldwide: hurricane damage in Charleston, SC.
Chapter 3 background © Pictor: Eiffel Tower in Paris, France.
Chapter 4 background © Weatherstock: hurricane winds bending trees.
Pp. 7, 10 © NASA/GSFC/JPL, MISR Science Team; p. 13 © Liam Gumley, Space Science and Engineering Center, Univ. of Wisconsin Madison; p. 14 © Macduff Everton/Image Bank; p. 15 © NASA/GSFC, NOAA; p. 16 © FPG International; p. 20 © Frank Siteman/Index Stock; p. 22 © Hubert Stadler/Corbis; p. 24 © Roger Ressmeyer/Corbis; pp. 25, 49–53 © Weatherstock; p. 26 © Index Stock; p. 30 © David Vincent Campbell; pp. 32, 46 © AP/Worldwide; p. 35 © Volvox/Index Stock; p. 40 © Image Bank; p. 43 © Omni Photo Communications, Inc.

Series Design and Layout

Geri Giordano